# WAS CANADA EVER CHRISTIAN?

PUBLICATIONS

By Brian C. Stiller
Editor-in-Chief of Faith Today

FAITH TODAY Publications is the publishing division of the Evangelical Fellowship of Canada.

Printed and bound in Canada by Hignell Printing.

Canadian Cataloguing in Publication Data
Stiller, Brian C.
    Was Canada ever Christian?

Essays originally written for the column Understanding
    Our Times, in FAITH TODAY.

ISBN 0-9695596-6-6

1. Christianity – Canada. I. Title.

FC95.4.S75 1996      209'.71      C96-900769-8
F1021.2.S75 1996

FAITH TODAY Publications
M.I.P. Box 3745
Markham, Ontario
Canada L3R 0Y4

*Dedicated To:*

*Dr. George Rawlyk (1935-1995)*

*who, as scholar, football player, professor, mentor and mobilizer, encouraged research into the reality and role of the evangelical church community in Canada. For those of us who were touched by his loving toughness and his expanding Christian witness, we now know better what it means to give our all in service to the Lord of life.*

# CONTENTS

# INTRODUCTION

D oes the question "Was Canada ever Christian?" matter? Some say that even if Canada was once a Christian nation, in today's pluralism, what matters is that Canada no longer be considered so. Others ask, "Who cares? Even if it was, the point is irrelevant because Canada no longer is Christian."

I view an understanding of our past as vital. For who we are today grows out of the roots of our past. Is it an accident that many, including the United Nations, see Canada as being the best country in which to live? I think not. Our sense of goodness and our values are derived from what was planted.

The case for our Christian heritage has increasingly been made by Canadian historians, encouraged and led by the late George Rawlyk, former historian at Queen's University, Kingston, Ontario. Before his death in 1995, Rawlyk, by his teaching, writing and encouraging of graduate students, pressed the point that Canada indeed has a very rich Christian tradition. The point, of course, is not to decide whether in some formal or technical sense Canada was Christian, but rather that the shaping of this country was very much influenced by Christian thought, leadership and institutions. This sense of the past and the germ ideas of our national being is then instructive for our leaders today and in pointing us toward future. My point simply is to encourage us to reflect on the foundation of our nation and not ignore those elements that have contributed so much to who we are.

This book is a compilation of essays written primarily for "*Understanding Our Times*," a column in FAITH TODAY, the bi-monthly news/feature magazine published by the Evangelical Fellowship of Canada. This forum has pushed me to develop my own thinking on what it means to serve Christ in this secular age.

I'm grateful to those who have edited these writings in their first life and for Audrey Dorsch in doing the final work for this publication. My hope is that Canadian Christians will engage our world as faithful witnesses of his loving, saving grace.

Brian C. Stiller

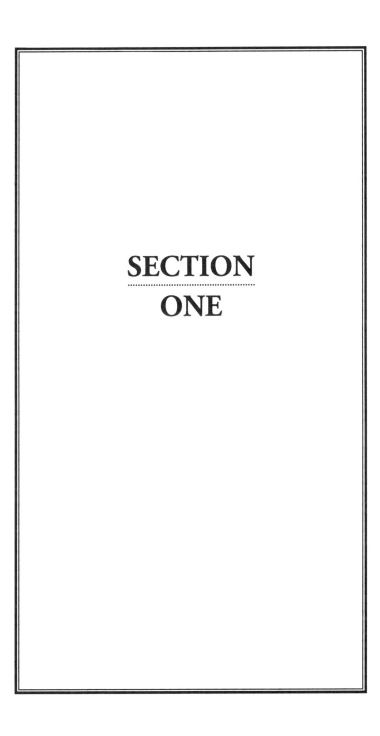

# SECTION
# ONE

# Was Canada ever Christian?

P eople often ask me, "Was Canada ever a Christian nation?" You may have heard that the United Nations said it no longer considered Canada as being Christian. I didn't believe that story, so we had it checked out. No, the UN never said that. As well, we know that most Canadians today still believe in a personal God. Up to two-thirds of Canadians believe that Jesus Christ is the Son of God. But it does seem as if Canada isn't as Christian as it once was.

However, as we accelerate to the end of this century, we do need to ask: What kind of Christian country do we pray for?

But first a word about being a Christian country. Former prime minister Pierre Elliot Trudeau said, "The golden thread of faith is woven throughout the history of Canada from its earliest beginnings up to the present time. Faith was more important than commerce in the minds of the European explorers and settlers."

When you drive through the villages of the St. Lawrence region you can see the historical influence of faith. In the middle of each settlement the local church, usually Catholic, Anglican or Methodist, is the dominant piece of architecture. You really can't understand Canada until you understand the central role the Christian faith had in the founding and shaping of Canada. But to say it was therefore a "Christian nation" calls for a look at the three main ways we use the phrase.

It can be used to mean a country with some connection to the Judeo-Christian heritage. Almost everything in Western culture from the late Roman Empire until 1800 was "Christian" in that sense, even though there were elements we would agree were not Christian.

The phrase can be used to mean a nation in which there are many individuals who claim to be Christian. But the presence of Christians in a country might only paint a picture of a country that is religious but not necessarily Christian. Consider, for example, South Africa. Most of the population confessed Jesus Christ, but the racial policies of apartheid imposed by the government were anything but "Christian."

The phrase can also be used to mean a society that reflects the ideals and principles of Scripture. That is, a country in which people are not just talking about doing God's will but are quite successful in doing it. I suppose this is the way we would want to use the term.

It is important that we make these distinctions. If we assume that political ideas and the Bible are the same, it is not a long step to idolatry and national self-righteousness.

As evangelicals become more proactive in political and social issues – which, I believe, is something born of the Spirit – it is important that we not be caught up in wishful thinking of a return to some glorious Christian moment of the past. I think too often our memory of Canada as being a "Christian nation" is caught up in either the first or second way we use the phrase.

I see two major ideas that can help to guide us as we engage our culture so that we are kept within earshot of Christ's call "to be in the world but not of it." These two are "corporate" Christianity – the Christendom model – and "individual" Christianity.

Corporate Christianity's first expression appeared in the fourth century when Emperor Constantine declared Christianity to be the official religion of the Roman Empire. In one stroke, Christianity changed from being an obscure sect that worshiped a Jewish rebel to a major world religion that sought to apply Christ's teachings to the political structure of the world's then-greatest power.

Though it was distorted and abused and was used to connect political and religious power, this expression of Christianity does remind us that a biblical vision of life for a nation has value.

The "individual" view of Christianity came out of the Reformation, which brought the understanding that God works in the hearts of individuals. Reformers such as Martin Luther, John Calvin and Menno Simons became major forces in the shaping of North American Christianity. At its heart, individual Christianity sees the relationship of the individual to God as being the most important expression of Christian experience.

These two views, corporate and individual, though seemingly in opposition, are never completely distinct. The combination of the two holds us in healthy tension. God does enter our hearts and does bring personal transformation and forgiveness. And he cares about the way in which we are ruled. It does matter to God that we live within a nationhood that blesses the people. King David understood that well: "Blessed is the nation whose God is the Lord," he said. Be wary of people who wish to return us to some former state wherein Canada was "Christian." They may be caught up in believing that by political force we can bring a spiritual rule. But also be wary of people who individualize faith so much that it has no concern whatever for the country.

Let us not misunderstand: the heart of this nation will be changed and renewed only when the people of God act like the people of God.

May our God rule Canada from sea to sea to sea.

## 2

# The Danger of Saying Canada was Christian

Anyone who might occasionally read one of my columns or hear me speak in a church will be surprised by this warning: It's dangerous to say Canada was a Christian nation.

Am I saying Canada was never Christian in its basic view of life? No. In fact, I often remind people of the enormous influence Christian faith has had on Canada. One cannot understand Canada without knowing the Christian leaders and ideas that have shaped this nation. With the work of Canadian historian Dr. George Rawlyk, among others, there is a growing body of historical analysis that shows the powerfully shaping presence of Christian life in the development of Canada.

For example, Egerton Ryerson, often cited as the father of our Canadian educational system, in his 1846 Report on a System of Public Elementary Instruction stressed "the absolute necessity of making Christianity the basis and cement of the structure of public education." Ryerson defended the presence of the Bible in schools as a "symbol of right and liberty dear ... to every lover of civil and religious liberty – a standard of truth and morals."

Yes, Canada is a country that rose out of a Christian – both Protestant and Catholic – vision of life. By any criteria for measuring the religious orientation of a nation, it can be said that Canada has a deep Christian tradition. This is not to say, of course, that have we always acted in a Christian way. I know the many stories of atrocities. Recall our unjust treatment of aboriginals and the way we exploited Chinese immigrants in building our national railway – a far cry from Christian principles. But our framework was still very much Christian.

If that is so, you ask, why is it dangerous to say Canada was a Christian nation?

We are vulnerable to being ruled by deep desires to return to the days of the past. Over the past few decades, Christian faith has been pushed from public life and our laws now ensure that our country is governed from a secular view of life. At the same time, the ability of churches to shape our public way of life has waned. This loss and the sense of being marginalized press us to call out for a return to the way we "remember" life in Canada.

There are dangers in that way of thinking. First, we may assume that our memories of the past are congruent with Christian orthodoxy. Second, we become trapped in trying to reinvent the past, believing that if we can reimpose the way we believe we once thought and acted, spiritual life will return. Third, we equate our past culture, which had a certain understanding of faith, with God's kingdom.

Historian Arnold Toynbee wrote, "We Christians . . . tend to treat Christianity as if it were the tribal religion of our particular civilization. In the West, we tend to treat it as something that derives its virtue not so much from being Christian as from being Western."

Reconstructing today out of memory is close to his warning of a relapse into worship of our past cultural patterns, believing they were godly for that time and are therefore godly for today. This "golden age" theory unfairly compares our memory of the past with the stark reality of the present.

If we dwell in this desire to return to the days of the past we deny, in effect, that God has an agenda for today and today's problems, an agenda that may be quite different from that of our parents' day. Look at the field of public education, for example. Though I wish we had more educators who are open to faith, as I recall we once had, the fact is we do not. Wishing it were so is far away from God's call to act today. So what do we do about it?

That's the critical issue. The gospel calls us to engage the world as we find it – not as we wish it were. The kingdom of our Lord is not trapped in the past. It is powerful, breaking down the idols of this age and uprooting the violent and untruthful ideologies of this culture. Nostalgia is okay when looking at the family album. But to influence our culture requires bold faith and a courageous heart, not to return to where we were but to move forward. Jesus said that anyone who when ploughing looks back is not worthy of the kingdom.

I understand well the deep feelings about the loss of our Christian roots. But spending time and energy wishing them back is both unproductive and antithetical to faith. Elijah, facing the prophets of Baal on Mt. Carmel, showed no interest in reminding the people of the good old days of Moses. Instead he employed God's provision in that encounter and "then the fire of the Lord fell."

Next time someone laments that Canada should be as it once was, remember that wishing to turn back the clock assumes God's kingdom is not adequate for today. "The gates of hell shall not prevail" is not a memory of the past. It is Jesus' promise for today.

## 3

# Will a Religious Right
# Rise in Canada?

Some Canadian journalists have become downright panicky over the rise of the religious right wing in the United States. They see in this American phenomenon a giant bogeyman of religious intolerance. They fear the loss of the liberal agenda of the past generation and the takeover of a conservative agenda. The logic is that if the religious right can rise in the United States, it might rise in Canada. "God forbid!" journalists would say.

The religious right is a powerful movement of politically and religiously conservative Americans who, out of angst over the moral drift of their nation, want to bring about change. Will the same movement occur in Canada? I sense that it won't, at least not in the same way. But that is not to say that there are not deeply felt concerns about a perceived moral drift in this country and a sense that Canadian Christians have been marginalized.

There are several reasons, though, why the religious right will not rise in Canada as it has in the United States:

• Canadians do not support the same "ideology of liberty" that drives American politics. This ideology leads to a resentment of government. Canadians view government as a servant, not an enemy. Though we Canadians celebrate our democratic rights, our understanding of human enterprise is expressed more in terms of community and less in terms of stark individualism and "freedom from" community.

• Canadian evangelicals are less conservative and less homogeneous in their politics than are Americans. During the 1992 presidential election, 72 percent of people who voted for Republican George Bush were self-declared "evangelical Protestants." During the 1994 federal election in Canada, 45 percent of all English-speaking evangelicals voted for the Progressive Conservative and Reform parties, and 45 percent voted for the Liberal Party. Evangelicals simply do not find themselves on one side or another of the political spectrum.

• Historically, and to a large degree still, the only strong correlation between a church community and a political party is the Roman Catholics with the Liberals. In the 1994 election 66 percent of Roman Catholics voted for the Liberal Party. Forty-seven percent of Canadians are Roman Catholic. In contrast, only 27 percent of the United States population is Roman Catholic.

• Conservative Protestants represent a larger proportion of the population in the United States than in Canada. The population of the United States is 10 times greater than Canada's; the number of conservative Protestants in America is 30 times larger than in Canada, however. In straight numbers, there are about 2.7 million evangelical Protestants in Canada compared to nearly 80 million in the United States. That huge number makes it easier in the United States than in Canada to raise money for political involvement and to exercise political leverage.

• There are proportionately more Mennonites in Canada than the United States, and in our country, they have had a moderating influence on political involvement by Canadian Christians. Mennonites tend to keep a distance from politics; when Mennonites do speak out on political matters, they support a moderate approach and generally do not identify with or promote "far-right" issues.

• There is no lingering belief here, as exists in the United

States, that Canada is a country destined by God to be the place in which his will and ways would be manifested. That notion contributes to powerful linkages of passionate nationalism and deeply held religious convictions. In contrast, Canadian nationalism is modest and, for most of us, not linked to a religious vision of the country.

• Compared to Americans, Canadians tend to be more "irenic," said the late historian George Rawlyk; that is, they promote peace. We didn't take the west by gun power, as the Americans did. We have not had a civil war. We did not achieve national independence by taking up arms. We don't burn down our inner cities as a means of protest.

Possibly our irenic nature derives from our being a relatively small population inhabiting a relatively vast area; it takes all of our cooperative efforts just to survive. Or possibly the division of our country into two major linguistic communities has forced us to find ways to live peacefully.

• The development of independent media forums in the United States, especially radio and television, has allowed the viewpoints of religious communities to be expressed among the public. Canada's regulatory body, the Canadian Radio-television and Telecommunications Commission, has suppressed such forums here until recently.

Without the huge population base to fund media enterprises, however, these forums for influence in Canada will be modest at best. Canadian Christians do not have access to the same communication vehicles as Americans to build commitment to their causes. Furthermore, mainstream Canadian broadcasters, for the most part, have treated Canadian evangelical movements, concerns and leaders with curiosity if not disdain.

Canadian evangelicals will continue to participate in politics, but in my view, it is unlikely that participation will ever approximate the participation of the religious right in American politics.

# 4

# Lament for a Prayer

On February 18, 1994, members of the House of Commons adopted a new morning prayer which, among other changes, dropped the name "Jesus Christ." The occasion produced a sense of sadness in me. I wrote to the prime minister, expressing my grief. Following is the essence of that letter:

With hardly a ripple of dissent, each Member of Parliament stood and agreed with the new, shorter and less stilted prayer.

One can hardly blame their quick, unmurmuring response. After all, living in a modern society comprising many faiths, how can a federal institution be so arbitrary in its wording as to exclude Canadians who profess faiths other than Christianity or who profess no faith at all? This change of prayer drew hardly a journalistic whisper, let alone a public outcry. It seemed so "Canadian" and so fair.

With the matter now legislatively behind us, I offer this lament because of the loss of something so inconspicuously grand. While we have flowed in the stream of multicultural and pluralistic fairness, we must not allow this event to pass without a reminder to us all of what has happened and what we have lost.

With one stroke of the legislative pen, we have cut out of our national daily offering of prayer what is to many the core of our vision of life and truth. I'm not suggesting that Canada was ever truly Christian or that our national or personal life has manifested fully the essentials of life in Jesus Christ. But it would be an enormous misreading of history not to recognize that our founders believed that a Christian vision of life was at the centre of this national experiment.

Nor is my lament for the passing of the old "Christendom" that was enforced in the past by the church establishment. That was never and is not how the gospel is worked out in life. Nor do I accuse the members of Parliament, suggesting they were part of a sell-out.

Rather, my lament is directed toward Christians who deeply and fervently believe that Jesus Christ offers to people an under-standing and way of life that is of benefit to all. This is our failure. We have not given evidence of what comes to a people who in thought and life emulate this teacher from Nazareth. Somehow in our living out his call, it has not become apparent to other Canadians that his ways bless a people.

The Angus Reid polls on religious attitudes in Canada demonstrate the high level of Christian faith among Canadians. Sixty-seven percent said that belief in the death and resurrection of Jesus Christ is essential for salvation. With this as a backdrop, why then would our legislatures so quickly drop any reference to the one whom two-thirds of Canadians say is central to faith and life? And why would there be almost no public response?

The answer lies in an ineffectual and watered-down faith. We as Christians are living out a life of faith that does not surprise, attract or compel. For some Christians, the Word of God has become merely a nice text of worthwhile quotables. How can we expect others to take seriously what some Christians aren't sure is true? For other Christians, who believe the truth of the Bible, the gospel has too often been privatized and hidden behind the doors of congregations and within the cloisters of private life.

Some argue that because Canada has a rich and profound Christian heritage, the country should be required to retain the symbols of that heritage. But life is not static. Symbols do not retain meaning without good reason. Christian symbols within our culture will be retained only as our culture is attracted to that faith.

One leader said that Christian prayers, be they in the House of Commons or in public schools, matter little. Minds wander, making the prayers both ineffectual and hypocritical. I am not interested in forcing people into perfunctory prayers. But the federal Parliament, our highest ruling body, has stripped from its vernacular an understanding of a transcendent God who in Jesus Christ visited this planet, giving flesh and substance to hope and life. Symbols teach us. They serve as a paradigm, a hermeneutic, a way of seeing all of life. When that is taken away, the ability to inform new generations is eroded.

While I grieve the loss of a prayer which made explicit reference to Jesus Christ in the federal Parliament, much more acute is the realization that we, his followers, have not lived out the compelling and culture-shaping life of the gospel. The long-term loss for Canada is great. But my lament is for Christians.

The story is told of a rabbi in Russia who complained to Catherine the Great about the mistreatment of Jews. The empress responded that maybe it was time for Jews to become Christians.

"No," said the rabbi, "it's time for Christians to live as Christians."

## 5

# A Religious Profile
# of Canada

In 1893, George Grant of Queen's University in Kingston, Ontario, spoke at the Congress on Religions in Chicago. Commenting on the state of affairs in Canada, he said all is well: the Sabbath is kept by Canadians and the gospel is held in high regard.

Using those two windows as a means of evaluating the strength of the Christian faith in Canada, today we would say the opposite of Grant's judgment. Sunday is now a day for sports and friends, and the gospel is seen by many as something only for one's private faith or the cloistered expression of a congregation.

If Grant were to parachute into Canada today, the shocking difference between our day and his would convince him that all had been lost. How often I hear people lamenting the loss of Christian faith in the culture. Indeed one can make the argument that, in terms of public influence, the Christian gospel has been secularized; that is, pushed to the side, ignored by the public rulers who deem it to have no relevance to modern Canadian living.

Dr. M.H. Ogilve, professor of law at Carleton University, has recently written that among Canadian Christians there is "a rising tide of apprehension, anger, a sense of betrayal and alarm at the speed with which the formerly Christian fabric of Canadian society has been unravelled with the half-generation since 1982 and certainly within the generation since 1968." She continues to say that "Canada, like the United States, seems to careening out of control, while its Èlites plunder their spiritual inheritance and increasingly deny its expression in everyday life."

Such analysis is shocking, especially from one whose vocation is spent in the analysis and teaching of law. And I concur. As I work on the national front, putting forward evangelical convictions on issues of public legislation, as we argue in the Supreme Court on some of the most critical ethical concerns of today, I face the cynicism and ridicule of an Èlite who are the cultural door-keepers of our culture.

As we look at the future of Canada and examine how our witness is to be made, I suggest there are two windows through which we can see our witness of Christ to the nation:

### *The Window of Public Witness*

Some say such concerns of witness in our parliaments and courts are outside the domain of the gospel. They argue that only the winning of individuals to faith in Jesus Christ is what we should be about. I differ. In 1994, the EFC was a co-intervenor in the Sue Rodriguez case; she was asking for court approval of doctor assisted-suicide. As we sat in the court listening to the various lawyers, including our counsel, make their case, it occurred to me that indeed at that moment in that auspicious place we were about the business of evangelism.

I mentioned this to a pastor who responded, "Brian, haven't you stretched the definition of evangelism too far?"

We then debated on how we define "evangelism." We eventually agreed that evangelism simply means to declare the evangel. Not a huge leap of logic there. So we went further. What is the evangel? We agreed it is the good news of Jesus. And what is that good news? It is that Jesus has come. And because he has come we see all of life differently.

Before the Supreme Court of Canada we reasoned that life and death are to be seen differently because of the evangel. Of course, our factum and legal counsel talked in language appropriate to the court setting. But at the heart of our intervention was a vision of life right out of the Bible. In the end, the majority decision, written by Justice John Sopinka, was based on "the sanctity of life," and although he argued that it was a "secular" view, our approach was to affirm that "sanctity" comes from a Christian vision of life.

Being in the courts today is an outworking of what it means to be a faithful witness of our risen Lord. Given the enormous power of the courts arising out of the Charter of Rights and Freedoms, we would be unfaithful to the body of Christ not to provide reasoned arguments for biblical values in that setting and in cases which are critical to the health and well-being of our culture. Also, if we aren't there, who will provide for them a Christian witness? The old legal maxim "use it or lose it" reminds us that, unless we are faithfully and consistently there, putting forward our Christian rationale, there is all likelihood it will never enter into the judges' thinking as they make their decisions.

Robert Nadeau, a good friend and lawyer, and one who provides us with good counsel wrote,

*Herein lies the challenge for the church. Pious detachment from matters of state and public policy is no longer a defensible option for the church in a pluralistic society. Issues of life, moral conduct, social justice and individual empowerment . . . are matters that must be nourished by spiritual direction, compassion and transcendent standards if they are to possess any enduring value. In the present context we would do well to remember that the rights enshrined in the Charter are really what we make them. And what we make of them depends ultimately on how seriously we take the commandment to be salt and light in a broken world.*

I would argue that it is in the interest of the Christians to so declare the good news in the public squares of our land so this nation will remain open to allow the public witness of Christ by way of Scripture and other means. A nation that sees itself within the framework of Judeo-Christian belief will be more hospitable to the open witness of Christ. There is an accumulative benefit to a nation whose underlying assumptions are biblical. To affirm those truths is, in my view, evangelism.

## *The Window of Personal Witness*

Vision 2000 Canada is the Evangelical Fellowship of Canada's Task Force on Evangelism. As we prepare for a new and courageous outreach, it is vital that we first understand the religious composition of Canada, the problems we face and the factors which encourage the church.

How Christian is Canada? The definition of "Christian" will depend on one's theology. An evangelical definition, for example, will be narrower than others. For our purposes it's important we examine this question from more than one angle.

There are three ways for we can examine the Canadian religious landscape:

• The census. First, let's use the term "Christian" in the broad sense: anyone who claims the name. The 1981 census shows that, out of a total population of 24,083,495 Canadians, 11,402,605 claim to be Catholic, 361,560 to be Eastern Orthodox and 9,914,580 Protestant. Thus 90 percent say they are Christian.

• Church attendance. Another way to examine people's Christian commitment is to ask how often they go to church. From that question, 27 percent of Protestants claim they have been to their place of worship within the past seven days, and 43 percent of Catholics and Eastern Orthodox the same. This indicates that, on average, 32 percent of Canadians attend a Catholic, Eastern Orthodox or Protestant church each week.

(Source: Reginald Bibby, *Fragmented Gods,* Irwin, 1987.)

• Evangelical belief. To narrow the religious analysis further, we can ask how many Canadians consider themselves to be evangelical Protestants. There are two major factors in answering this responsibly: (1) Protestant churches that publicly affirm their evangelical commitment, and (2) individuals who consider themselves evangelical but attend a mainline church that does not identify itself as being "evangelical."

According to the 1981 census, two million Canadians list themselves as belonging to an evangelical church. Though there are no statistics to tell us how many within the mainline Protestant churches (Anglican, Lutheran, Presbyterian and United Church) would consider themselves evangelical. In examining this with Dr. Bibby, we concluded that six percent, or nearly 463,000, of those attending main-line Protestant churches (7,709,400) are of evangelical faith.

Adding those totals we estimate (and it is at best an estimate) 2.5 million Canadians – representing about 10 percent of Canadians – affiliate with evangelicalism by belief and/or by regular attendance at an evangelical church.

These statistics are only a partial picture, however. We know only too well that many are "nominal evangelicals" in that, though they may identify with being evangelical and affirm their belief in the Scriptures, their lives bear no evidence of saving faith. Thus, while nine out of ten Canadians believe in a personal God, seven out of ten believe that Jesus Christ is the son of God and 32 percent attend church with some form of regularity, other indicators show that Canada is in desperate need of spiritual renewal.

### *The Problems we Face*

In targeting for outreach in Canada, there are specific problems we face. To make any significant impact, its vital that we seriously examine them.

Next to the Soviet Union, Canada has the largest land mass in the world. Yet our population is no larger than that of California. Spread out over nearly 10 million square kilometres incorporating six regions, Canada is divided by regional self interest, diverse languages, ethnic links and economic problems. This sprawling effect makes it difficult for religious waves to generate momentum.

Although we live on the edge of the highly religious United States, when you attempt to speak to the average Canadian about his or her spiritual life, it is like asking about one's sex life. Matters of personal concern, like spirituality, are not seen as something one talks about casually with a relative stranger. Thus, evangelistic methods that rely on making an approach about faith in Christ in a relatively short time after initial contact will struggle.

Large meetings are not nearly as popular as they are in the nation to the south. Sports is a prime example. Canadians, although very much in love with hockey, do not, as a rule, congregate in large numbers. Thus our use of mass crusades, though certainly valuable, has not had the impact it has elsewhere.

Canadian religious roots are largely Roman Catholic (Canada is 47 percent Catholic) and Church of England. Given that evangelism has used a more emotional approach, the reaching of nominal Catholics or Anglicans has not been very effective.

Critical to the strategy of reaching our nation is leadership. There are two reasons why this is an issue. The Canadian style is in general, more laid back and less assertive than, for example, that of Americans. Though this has certain advantages, the community comes to expect church leaders, in their "servant" role, not to give direction. Also, many capable leaders are attracted to the greener fields of the U.S. This is true of the church as well as other vocations. As well, we have so few Christian liberal arts universities in Canada. Many students thus attended

American schools, such as Wheaton, married, found jobs and stayed. Today we are attempting to raise a new generation of spiritual leaders who are willing to remain in Canada and not bow to the cultural pressure of those who assume that leadership is just fulfilling the wishes of others.

For the past quarter century, secularization has taken over as the fundamental assumption of our culture. During the early part of this century, when secularity was emerging as a national force, evangelicals were trapped by the sectarianism of fundamentalism. As a result we were unable to venture forth in cultural renewal and the Canadian public arena was depleted of its Christian assumptions. The result is that we now face a community which asserts that Christian faith is to be kept private.

Seldom in Canadian history have we seen a sustained, widespread move of God. The most remarkable revival occurred in the Atlantic region in the early 1800s. Led by Henry Alline, the New Light movement was used to bring many into a living relationship with Christ. In the early 1970s Saskatoon witnessed a brief but locally contained revival. There is much talk and praying for revival yet little is known of its cost or impact in a Canadian context.

Canada lacks a publishing base and, in my view, this is important. Almost all of the books that find their way into our studies and homes are published in the United States or United Kingdom. In simple terms this means that most of the analysis and ideas come from those who live elsewhere and do not understand our issues and circumstances. As well, there is little encouragement for the development of indigenous writers who reflect and stimulate thinking in a national context.

## Is There Hope?

Though these peculiar challenges confront us in evangelizing Canada, we are reminded of the many opportunities and signs of encouragement. We believe that as we are faithful there will be a blossoming of spiritual life in the nation, such as we have never witnessed.

Canadians continue to believe in the transcendent and in Jesus as the Christ. Although this faith tends to be nominal, it does remind us that, in general, Canadians are not atheists. The rise of the New Age movement is another reminder that even the socially sophisticated and academically inclined will open their minds to religious ideas.

Canadians tend to support national networks, and denominations are our prime religious networks. Although there has been a modest independent church movement, even those tend to cluster in groups. This provides quick access to the various churches and groups.

This country struggles with social problems as do all nations. One of our tragedies is the native situation. But our cities are not plagued with the same inner city desolation, crime and poverty as are American cities. This allows us to use our resources to concentrate on church growth and outreach. The danger, however, is that with a strong governmental structure the work of social reconstruction and beneficial services are pushed off to government.

Television is both a blessing and curse. The world has come to know of the failings of certain evangelists. We live on the border of a nation where unbridled religious speakers flourish, and television cable systems pump that religious material into our homes; the failings of specific personalities make quite a noise. Canadian televangelists, for the most part, have maintained a high reputation for financial and moral integrity. Their faithful testimonies have brought a credibility to the gospel.

Basic to our evangelical educational community has been the Bible school movement. Their contribution to the spiritual welfare of this nation has been outstanding, for out of this community have come our pastors and missionaries. The biblical focus of these institutions moulds the lives of our prime spiritual care givers. And for that we are blessed.

One quarter of Canadians speak French as their first language. The majority live in Quebec. In the early 1960s, a social and political revolution erupted. Beginning in that difficult time, a most remarkable of spiritual movement has developed. Churches are being built such as Anglophones never expected.

Another area of outreach and church growth is among the newer ethnic communities, specifically among Chinese, Korean and other Asian peoples. Churches are springing up under the leadership of their own people.

What I find most encouraging is the evident desire for cooperation. As noted, Canada is plagued with the "balkanization" problem; our country is divided by geography, language, and regional self interest. Under the pressure of this cultural tendency, younger and older leaders are resisting disunity, looking for ways to cooperate and fellowship. This is nothing short of historical.

The most significant sign of hope, however, is the increased desire for prayer. Never have I witnessed Canadians talk about the need for prayer, organize prayer gatherings and spend time in prayer as they do today.

While the forces of secular individualism attempt to marginalize the gospel, within the hearts of Canadian believers there is a new cry for the purifying presence of Christ.

Two questions I ask. Are we prepared for the personal sacrifice required for spiritual rebirth and do we have any idea what will result when King Jesus indeed rules and reigns?

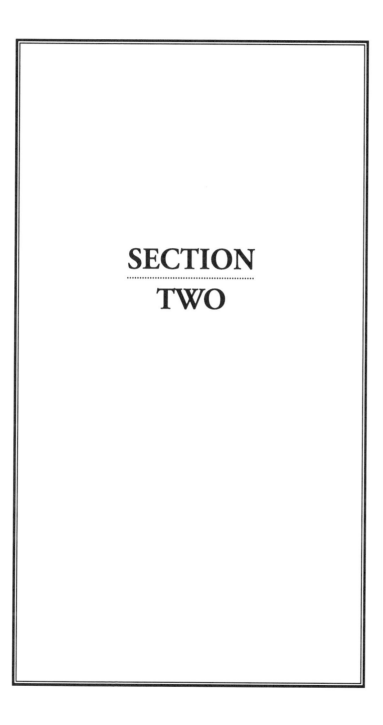

# SECTION
## TWO

## 6

# Other War Heroes

The 50th anniversary of Victory in Europe Day overlooked one very important person. As the celebrations wove their way up and down the streets of towns and villages in the Netherlands, as the bands played and wreaths were laid at memorials in parks across northern Europe and the United Kingdom, I looked in vain for a mention of a valiant voice of truth within the evil thunder of the war of 1939-45.

I too celebrated the liberation of the Dutch by Canadian troops. I felt the great wash of emotion as Hollanders, now older, hugged and danced with Canadian war veterans. I too brushed away tears as I heard stories of the Allies, and especially Canadians, as they gave their lives to shut down the Nazi wave. I, too, saw the old film footage of horror, violence and unspeakable evil of unrestrained nationalism. But I did not hear a mention of another person, whose 50th anniversary I remembered.

It was the remarkable German theologian and pastor Dietrich Bonhoeffer, who died for his faith 50 years ago. At dawn on April 9, 1945, his life was cut short by a Nazi noose. He had risen against the evils of Nazism and spoken in uncompromising terms and for that his life was taken while others of his colleagues drowned in a sea of compromise to the grand and powerful Nazi machine.

It is appropriate to celebrate the Allied victory. The huge

investment of young lives that Canada and our allies made in restraining evil is important for us to remember. As a Cub in the Boy Scouts, each year I marched and stood before the cenotaph in Saskatoon, learning the importance of remembering our fallen soldiers. They gave their lives to stave off the ruthless hobnail boots of totalitarianism; it was and still is vital that we remember and by so doing learn the lessons of that time.

Older now, as I watch the veterans of the wars I have deep and lingering respect for the suffering and horror they went through to sustain a vision of goodness and rightness.

Within these celebrations, however, I looked for even a modest acknowledgement that within Hitler's sinister domain too, someone rose in resistance.

Early in his life Dietrich Bonhoeffer was interested in theology and faith. Beginning as a professor, he eventually saw his true calling as that of pastor. But a quiet pastoral life was not to be his. Amid the radical and racist nationalism of Hitler, he was called to take a stand and lead others to see past the excitement of the so-called miracle worker. Bonhoeffer discerned the evil of this rising German empire in his fatherland and began to voice strong opposition during a time in which most church leaders were knuckling under to the wishes of the Fuhrer.

Bonhoeffer's concerns led him to join with the Confessing Church, founded in 1933 by Pastor Martin Niemoller. They wrote and signed the famous Barmen Declaration, which laid the basis for the resistance against the Nazis' attempt to make the Evangelical Churches an instrument of Nazi policy. By this document they outlined their deep opposition to extreme nationalism and the subjugation of the gospel of Christ to political power. Eventually the Nazis forbade Bonhoeffer to preach and removed him from his teaching post.

When the war broke out, Bonhoeffer was in North America on a preaching tour. He knew what faced him if he returned, but he believed God was calling him to return. He could not imagine staying away from his Christian colleagues when they were undergoing such oppression.

He did return and in 1943 was arrested and imprisoned by the Gestapo at Flossenburg. In 1945, he was hanged.

For me, the most powerful of his writings are contained in his book *The Cost of Discipleship*, much of which was written while he was in prison. I recall that as I was starting out in ministry, Bonhoeffer's powerful words caught my attention: when God calls you, he calls you to die. Not the kind of soft-selling religious clatter we too often hear today.

Whenever we remember and learn from the atrocities of war, let us also remember and learn from this young German pastor and theologian who left the ivory tower of academia, who left the protection of North America, returning home to what he surely knew would lead to his death. He courageously planted the flag of biblical faith in front of the marching maniacs of the Gestapo.

Though the victory of the Allies over Germany is an event to be celebrated, we are to be reminded, as the Old Testament prophet needed to be reminded, that there were many within the system who did not bow the knee to Baal.

## 7

# Being in a Place
# to Influence

I have wondered about why biblical faith has lost influence as a shaper of Canadian culture. As Canada entered the 20th century, we came out of a century that Canadian historian Michael Gauvereau called *The Evangelical Century* (in his book by that title). His careful analysis describes the enormous influence that evangelical Protestant theology and leadership had on Anglo-Canadian life. Why have we lost that place during this century?

There are many reasons for this loss. Some of these reasons include:

**1.** The takeover of mainline Protestant theology by a liberal view of Scripture, called "higher criticism."

**2.** The influence of Darwin's theory and accompanying science-related movements.

**3.** The rise of the "social gospel" and the consequent interpretation of salvation to mean the saving of society, not the individual.

**4.** The shift of evangelicals toward a theology called premillennialism, in which the expectation of the immediate return of Christ was central to the beliefs of many of the newly developing 20th-century evangelical churches and denominations.

The result was that the evangelical community from the early part of this century through to the 1980s exercised little or no opportunity of speaking biblical faith into the culture.

My point is not to provide a full explanation for this loss but to point out that during this distancing of our churches and theology from the running of this country, we were perceived in a particular way. As we withdrew and increasingly made our faith private, preaching a gospel that was directed only to individual conversion and the preparing of people for heaven, we viewed the surrounding world as unworthy of our interest or attention.

More and more we looked at society as being already condemned by God. This view tended to push evangelical leaders and congregations away from understanding our country's need for God-centred leadership. But what did this distancing do to the way non-evangelicals saw us?

In 1925, the impact of a public trial in Tennessee rippled its way north into Canada. Two lawyers, Clarence Darrow and William Jennings Bryon, faced each other in a dispute over state laws that prohibited the teaching of evolution. School teacher John Scopes triggered the court action by teaching evolution. The anti-evolutionists, defended by Bryon, won the case, but the media made it into the "Scopes monkey trial" and used it to discredit the evangelical cause. This only added to a public perception that people who believed the Bible were not only anti-social but anti-intellectual. In such an environment, Bible believers were viewed as having nothing to offer.

In the '40s and '50s, our strident anti-community and anti-liberal message made us appear angry. The rise of various prophetic formulas increased our pessimism about society, which in turn translated into a further distancing of our sense of responsibility from the needs of Canada.

Now, five or six decades later, we ask why our biblical message has been ignored and rejected. But should we be surprised? How would we expect a political leader, high school principal or newspaper reporter to respond to a group of people who seem angry and rejecting? Though these stereotypes may be unfair, the cultural gate-keepers viewed us as being at odds with the concerns of society, seemingly always in reaction without any expression of concern to find answers or provide solutions.

As we move into the last years of this millennium there are two critical issues at stake. First is a biblically driven concern for the promise of Christ's return. At the heart of the message of the kingdom is that in God's appointed schedule, time as we know it will be wrapped up into eternity. Life is not a cycle, moving through a repetition of events with no ultimate conclusion. His kingdom will not be realized by improving life around us. Sin and evil will be finally defeated by the fullness of Christ's rule and reign.

But such a focus does not exclude a deep concern for witness within society. The very words describing Christ – "Saviour" and "Lord" – imply that his message and presence cover all of life. Jesus refused to allow his message to be disconnected from life. Our inclination has been to divide the spiritual world from the physical world.

Christ used three metaphors to describe our witness: "salt," "light" and "yeast." They imply that his kingdom is centred in the world to preserve, to illumine and to permeate. The work of the kingdom will be done as members of the kingdom are filled with enthusiasm and love in preserving, illuminating and permeating all of life.

To live in expectancy of Christ's return does not mean one has to live in anger and hostility to the people and issues of our generation. Neither does caring about life mean one is not living with an eye to his coming.

There is nothing especially valuable in having society despise our stand or view us as hostile. Yes, we will stand in opposition to the ways of evil. But let us be reminded that Jesus drew to himself those searching for love and truth.

If we are committed to shaping our nation with biblical values, we need to set aside the angry, hostile reaction and give evidence of God's goodness in redeeming the lost, forgiving the fallen, loving the unlovely and freeing those in bonds.

Holding in tension our hope of his coming and obedience to his calling, we can attract the hearts of Canadian leadership to Christ.

# 8

# The Babel Syndrome: Speaking Truth in Confusion

F ollowing Noah a civilization grew in Babylon which, like Noah's generation, fell into trouble. They built in Babel a tower, the writer of Genesis records, that reached to the heavens (Gen. 11:4). On the surface, this project in Babel appeared to be a noble one – something of a large-scale urban renewal project providing people with homes and places of work. The building of the tower sprang from less than dignified motives however; all they wanted to do was "make a name for ourselves." (Gen. 11:4)

Contravening God's command "to be fruitful and multiply and populate the earth . . . and multiply in it" (9:7) they chose the opposite, to remain together and accumulate power. By confusing their language, God brought a wall between them. But for what purpose? To prevent the accumulative power of consensual evil. The concentration within one group would by centripetal force – that is, by driving toward the centre – intensify evil to such a magnitude as to cause the community to self-destruct.

The confusion of language had the opposite effect. It acted as a centrifugal force, driving people away from the centre, thus breaking up the convergence of evil. In the breaking up of the human race into linguistic groups, the colossal evil of this large, unified group was minimized. In this process, human existence was preserved. Confusion, in the end, saved them.

A few thousand years later, God used language with a reverse purpose, as on the Day of Pentecost Christ introduced a unity as people from diverse languages heard the gospel in their own tongues.

## The Babel Metaphor

Our struggle to find an identity is made difficult by our unending squabble over language. And it's not something recent. Lord Durham, in his report to the British parliament in 1837, threw up his hands in frustration. "I found two nations warring within the bosom of a single state; I found a struggle, not of principles, but races" he wrote.

In the heat of today's political situation, with referendums and the threat of separation, language matters. I recall fire-side conversations as a boy; my father's relatives determined that the best solution for what language we would speak in heaven was to make it Swedish!

But our culture is caught in more than just a debate over linguistic usage or national self-definition. We are trapped by a culture that tells us what vernacular we can or cannot use. In this age of secular and materialistic scientism, religious language has no place in our public life. It has been muted, if not denied, in the public square of this land.

The dominant and all-embracing language of secular individualism has effectively screened out of public discourse conversations about faith. Peter Downy on a recent CBC radio show called *Tapestry*, asked me why there was so little faith talk in Canadian public life. He observed that there are very few occasions when mainstream media take faith seriously.

Stephen Carter, professor of law at Yale, in *The Culture of Disbelief* wrote, "More and more, our culture seems to take the position that believing deeply in the tenants of one's faith represents a kind of mystical irrationality, something that thoughtful public-spirited American citizens would do better to avoid."

Yes, there is little conversation about faith in our public square. In this century, science has written the sacred cannon and published the commandments: The Scientific Method. Research, faith or ideas not able to make it through its grid or survive its scrutiny are declared irrational or false. Faith, becomes quaint or curious.

For a good part of this century we have all worshipped at these shrines. Now, at the end of this millennium, we return to face the deep and troubling questions about ultimacy, truth and eternity. Epistemology (meaning the way we know and understand), shoved for too long on the back burner, is being pushed to the front, not by the scholars who earn their bread by its fare, but by common people who ask what it means to be human and wonder how, as a creature of this creation, one can be in touch with life and creation. Quite a contrast to Freud, who saw faith as a crutch.

A reporter from *Maclean's* magazine asked me if our view of creation had been disturbed by the discoveries on the Big Bang theory. Scientists report they have been able to listen back into the moment of the beginning of physical matter. The question they asked was, "Does this upset your views of creation?"

"No, indeed the opposite," I responded. "It is remarkable that modern man is forced to kneel in humility, admitting that the theories of the eternalness of matter were wrong. Now they are forced to confess there was a time when matter did not exist. This matches my understanding of the Genesis creation story, reinforcing the validity, even in scientific terms, of believing in a creator God."

I concluded: "The scientist was right when he said he felt he was looking in the face of God."

The Babel syndrome is not just hostility to spiritual language. We have been numbed by the trivial and superficial language of entertainment. Rex Murphy, the Canadian iconoclast, in reflecting on the annual Oscars, wondered about the intelligence of a people who calibrate the "minuscule superiorities that distinguish Tom Hanks as a moron, from John Travolta as a Hood." He reminded us that "a civilization with Hollywood as its crown deserves to be extinct."

I interpret the Babel syndrome as a cultural assumption that nothing is true: that all truths are relative, with each making its own contribution but unable to say anything certain. In Francis Schaeffer's words, something which is "truly true."

Three baseball umps being interviewed by a reporter about their profession were asked how they call balls and strikes.

The first said, "There are balls and strikes and I calls them as they are."

The second one differed. "There are balls and strikes and I calls them as I sees them."

The third one shook his head, "They ain't nothin 'til I calls them."

That's relativism. Nothing is "truly true." Something is only true if is true to you. And objectively, truth is impossible.

It's into that world we come as people of Christ's Kingdom.

### The Language we Bring

Out of our evangelical history and heritage we come with a language rich in meaning. We take the Bible as being true. The words of faith are more than ideas; they are power. "It is the power of God for the salvation of everyone who believes," Paul wrote (Rom. 1:16). Language is more than words to us. It is God in life and action. He reminds us, "For it is with your heart that you believe and are justified, and it is with your mouth that you confess and are saved." (Rom. 10:10).

But can we go beyond that? Are we able to so integrate our faith and words that we can speak to those who are not of faith? My fear is we have grown up in a sort of bifurcated world in which we speak words of faith in our church setting but, because we have difficulty translating into a language people understand, when we get out into the broader world we simply shut up.

Yes, in public life – be it media, our justice system, public education or public policy – the language of faith is absent. But is that because of a conspiracy? Is there a plan to make sure our faith is kept off the agenda? Although we have a Supreme Court decision that disallows faith from directly shaping public policy and a court ruling that eliminates Bible reading and prayer in public schools, claiming that it contravenes the Charter of Rights and Freedoms, culturally, on a broad scale I see no organized conspiracy. It's just that the cultural door-keepers have been caged by the prevailing ideologies: faith is private; it's not rational and is not important.

The issues now calling attention to our moral bankruptcy come from ethical questions for which there seem to be few answers. In recent years, we have floundered from courts to parliaments, searching for answers to life and death issues: from Sue Rodriguez on doctor-assisted suicide to Robert Latimer, the Saskatchewan farmer who took his daughter's life. I heard a justice in court ask a colleague in a stage whisper what foundation we have for moral values. It was tragic and pathetic.

So why the Babel syndrome, this confusion of language? Is it because modern ideologies build their temples of power? Is that what drowns out the language of faith? That's the common perception among many Christians. You've heard the argument: "We aren't allowed to speak. We're denied an opportunity."

I think we're wrong, although I've made the same assumption. That is, until in doing research for a book I was alerted to the sad reality that a century ago the articulators of evangelical Protestant faith themselves began to lose the language of faith. As the noise of secular language increased, especially following World War II, those voices we trusted to speak faith into the culture lost their determination and conviction. In the end, they had nothing to say and no will with which to speak.

It's tragic, but a sober reminder to us all. Whining about being shut out will get us no where and it's out of keeping with the very nature of the kingdom of our Lord. Furthermore, we were complicit in this loss of faith. We were absent. As those who had spoken for God stopped doing so, those of us who believed in the power of the gospel were so caught up in private individualism, focused on personal conversion as being the only way God speaks his truth into life, that we didn't even recognize the silence. Those who did shrugged it off as another sign that we were living in the end times, which meant there was nothing we could or should do.

## *A Great Moment of Opportunity*

In the midst of this Babel syndrome of confusion, the Spirit of God our creator brings healing, unity and truth by his kingdom. In the public square in which faith is absent we are called to speak a new language, a language of the Spirit and for this age. But for us to speak that language it calls us to learn a language of public discourse, to speak biblical faith and truth in ways that the public to which we speak understands.

Many of us have been blessed by the surroundings of our Christian families, churches and communities. Now we must become strategic, focusing our gifts and callings on specific communities into which God may lead.

A language of public discourse involves three realities:

• First, a deep conviction that God cares about all of life. "For by him all things were created: things in heaven and on earth, visible and invisible, whether thrones or powers or rulers or authorities; all things were created by him and for him." (Col 1:16)

• Second, a full and integrated faith in the power of our risen Saviour and Lord to bring healing, reconciliation and life.

• Third, a vision of God's call to his people to exercise

leadership in the public squares of this land. The kind of vision which will enable us to speak a language of public discourse: a language filled with God's truth but one which is both understood and is courageous to engage our contemporaries in the demanding issues of this age.

On Palm Sunday, we remembered the remarkable life of theologian and pastor Dietrich Bonhoeffer, who died for his faith fifty years ago. He rose up against the evils of Nazism. He was hung at dawn on April 9, 1945. He spoke with a language rooted in his risen Lord and focused on the raging conflict of his generation. He sent a message to the Bishop of Chichester, George Bell: "Tell him that for me this is the end but also the beginning."

He spoke the language of public discourse: his generation was not in the least misunderstanding of what he said. But there is something else: he added his life to his words.

John Updike, in *Seven Stanzas at Easter* writes:

*Let us not mock God with metaphor,*
*analogy, side stepping transcendence,*
*making of the event a parable, a sign painted in*
*the faded credulity of earlier ages.*
*Let us walk through the door.*

Let us defy the Babel syndrome. Let us walk through the doors into the public worlds of this age, speaking a language which resonates with our world, but always in the clear language of faith, hope and truth.

Winning over the grave is a language any one can understand.

# 9

# The Law as a Teacher

It was Tuesday morning, November 1, 1994. I left my Ottawa hotel room early to be sure of getting a seat in the Supreme Court. I had a hunch there might be a crowd; I was not disappointed. As I walked up the stairs of the grand structure, I could see that a line had already formed. The case that day was a challenge by James Egan who, along with his lover, was disputing the definition of "spouse" in the Old Age Security Act. At issue was whether Canadian law should retain the distinction between married/common-law opposite-sex couples and same-sex couples.

The EFC, with partners including Focus on the Family and the Canadian Conference of Catholic Bishops, had been given status to be intervenors. We were unsure whether the federal government would mount a strong case to defend a heterosexual basis for defining a spouse.

The courtroom filled and the justices filed in. We listened to legal positions, questions by the justices and counter arguments from the lawyers. Faces in the visitors' section reflected fears and hopes. We all knew that history was being made that day. All the work being done by various groups across Canada to protect a biblical vision of marriage could be lost in one Supreme Court ruling.

The lawyers and intervenors supporting the Egan case began.

Finally it was time for the government to defend the current law, which defines marriage as comprising two people of opposite sex. It was deeply disappointing to see the government's weak and ineffective defence. I was appalled at the seeming lack of preparation and knowledge. It was obvious that the arguments were not convincing the justices. I could hear sniggering as people realized the lawyer was in trouble. It was disconcerting that the representation for the side we were defending was incompetent.

As I listened to the arguments, it seemed that since the government had announced legislation to include sexual orientation in the federal Human Rights Act, it was not going to go out of its way in this case to defend the heterosexual meaning of marriage.

Then it was our turn as the Inter-Faith Coalition on Marriage and Family. Our legal counsel, Peter Jervis, stood and with obvious competence, clarity and a command of the issues spoke to the nine justices sitting before him.

I could see the justices take a new interest. Jervis's arguments cut to the core of the issue. His answers to the justices' questions were clear and to the point. All of a sudden the mood in the court chambers seemed to change.

During a break, a CTV reporter asked why we were so concerned about a few people who want their same-sex relationships defined as marriage. The assumption was that since it is such a small group, why should we even worry?

I responded by using Paul's reminder in Romans 7:7 that the law is a teacher. (Of course, I didn't tell the reporters my source.) I said that people come to believe that what is in the law is a statement of what is true. If you have untruth in law, then people come to believe that. If you have truth in law, citizens accept that. For us as Christians, the most critical aspect of this entire debate is upholding what we believe is biblically normative. And this means working to ensure that our laws reflect that.

Thus, we were in the Supreme Court to speak to what will

become our law, articulating what we believe is good for society. Traditionally, Parliament set the rules and the Supreme Court refereed them. Since our country shifted toward the American approach in 1982 with the adoption of the Charter of Rights and Freedoms, the courts in effect set laws by their rulings. We have no means of speaking into the process of decision making unless we are present in the courts. It is as simple as that.

At the end of that Tuesday, we thanked the Lord for the opportunity to intervene in the case. If we had not been there with tough and useful arguments, only the weak case of the federal government would have been put forward.

What a powerful reminder of the reason such a voice is needed in Canada. It is not enough to believe you have good answers. You have to gain a position at the table, to earn recognition that as a community you have something to say. When Paul appealed to be heard by Caesar, he accessed the highest court to the end that his account of the good news might be heard.

## 10

# Learning to Speak to Public Issues

I n an interview, Peter Downey of the CBC radio show *Tapestry* asked why public life is devoid of religious talk. His question called to mind a book, *The Culture of Disbelief.* Written by Stephen Carter, professor of law at Yale University, it probes this same question, which is at the heart of our modern culture.

Carter's interest is in "what religiously devout people should do when they confront state policies that require them to act counter to what they believe is the will of God, or to acquiesce in conduct by others that they believe God forbids." He contends that our cultural leaders say, "Do nothing."

That is the most complex and yet focused issue of this generation: what should we say when state policies run across the grain of our church or personal faith? Furthermore, how should we state our position?

First, a look at how we lost religious engagement in the public square: five primary reasons our society no longer allows faith-loaded conversation in public policy discussion or in the leadership of public life.

At the turn of this century the Western world was caught up in the glories of science. Theories of Darwin (natural science), Freud (psychology), Adam Smith (economics) and Max Weber (sociology) created an illusion that religious ideas are acceptable only when they conform to the scientific method. This holus-bolus acceptance of science as the final arbitrator of truth put a spiritual head-lock on us for most of this century.

In concert with this was a rejection of spiritual life as having any legitimacy except within church or personal experience. Freud created the delusion that faith was unreliable and thus unacceptable as an influence in issues as important as public life.

Along with this was the radical division of Protestant thinking and faith. While liberal theology seduced some early 20th-century Protestants (including some, but not all, within the Anglican, Congregational, Methodist, Presbyterian and Lutheran churches), the conservative reaction produced a sectarian, withdrawn grouping out of which many of this century's evangelical churches emerged. The resulting realities: old-line churches gradually lost their ability to speak with biblical and moral authority into the culture and the evangelical minority had no interest. In English-speaking Canada this ended up in profound public silence.

These factors fed into the process we now call secularization, aided by an economic factor, consumerism. Following World War II, the ability to buy on credit pushed our society into a preoccupation with the new idol: the shopping centre.

This resistance to things spiritual is even more apparent in Canada than in the United States. On *Larry King Live* (CNN), Congressional House Speaker Newt Gingrich said he was impressed, while looking at the Lincoln Memorial, that God had called him to this great nation. If Preston Manning dared to utter such a reflection publicly, the press and political pundits would tear him to shreds. Though there is ridicule in the United States over faith language in public discourse, it is considered more legitimate there than here in Canada.

The result? Issues of faith are not only discredited but denied entry. Moreover, often those who hold the cultural keys of public discourse argue that since our world is pluralistic, matters of faith – especially those of people who view their way as the only way to God – should be off the table.

So back to the question posed by Peter Downey and Stephen Carter about how we live in a world in which our faith is contradicted and the culture says, "Keep quiet; say nothing."

There are three steps Christian can take to open the doors of public life to biblical truth and Christ-centred saltiness:

The first is to learn a language of public discourse which both speaks the truth of Christ and does so in words understood in the public forum. We do not need religious-sounding words to speak religious truth.

Then we must find ways to be at the table. There is no better way to speak into the public debate than to be there. The other evening on television, Sue Careless, a parent concerned with homosexual sex education in public schools, debated the issue on CBC's *Face Off.* It was tough and she was under attack. But her courage kept her there. And she was credible.

Third, we need to offer ideas, not moralize. To moralize means to debate another's views by saying they are bad or evil. In the end, to do this in public debate not only discredits our arguments but does disservice to our witness of Christ. It is fine to moralize in church, but in public debate we hurt our ability to persuade if we get distracted into name-calling or moral denunciations. Alternative ideas call people's attention to consider a way out.

*The Globe and Mail* in a recent editorial admitted the need for including faith issues within our public debate: "The integration of values and spirituality into politics will not be easy."

I hear a faint call out of the bankruptcy of our culture for a word of faith. This is an enormous call and a historic opportunity to affirm that the kingdom of Christ speaks to all of life.

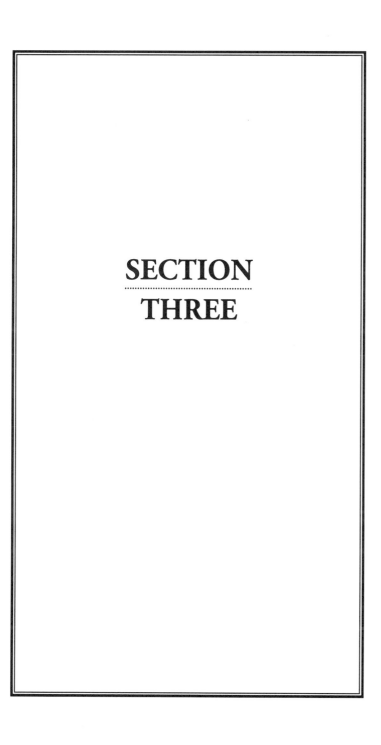

# SECTION
# THREE

# 11

# Think Before we Die

The waves of sympathy and respect for Sue Rodriguez camouflaged the real issue at stake in this debate: should a person be allowed to help another commit suicide?

I respect the courage and dignity Rodriguez displayed in advocating her point of view. Her claim for autonomy resonates with the commonly held assumption that our bodies are our own and we should be able to do with them as we want.

At the heart of this debate, however, is an understanding of what we have commonly understood to be the meaning of murder. To avoid using the word is to pretend the debate is not about that. If we wish to redefine the word and move the boundaries of what our law defines as murder, then we must as a society understand that that is what we are doing.

The Constitution and Criminal Code both act as mirrors, reflecting what we as Canadians believe. We have laws to protect life and laws that punish those who injure or end life. To now say, "We'll allow you, on the basis of someone's request, to end a life" is a departure from what we as a society have held. If we give courts the latitude to confer on people the right to authorize someone else to assist them in taking their own lives, it means that as a society our views of life have radically changed.

The assumption that our lives are just our own – meaning it's not the business of anyone else what we do with them – is a classic Enlightenment view. It focuses on the autonomous, unhindered will of the individual. But this belief runs smack into the wall of a growing realization that individualism as a ruling ideology is counter-productive and in the end has a disintegrating affect on society.

Liberal individualism, though promoting self-asserted action, cannot obscure the fact that we are not islands, living without regard for each other. What one person does affects others. Our laws, health care system and educational institutions are run on the assumption that we are not John Waynes, striding off into the horizon, accountable only to self. As humans, we are incredibly interrelated and interdependent.

Further, to expect medical professionals to be responsible for deciding how to respond to a patient's request for help in suicide is to distort the very nature of their calling. What does this do to their vows of preserving life? Do we make them into state-supported life terminators?

In the face of dominant secularism, Canadians are showing a remarkable resilience in spirit-centred concerns. Issues of meaning, ultimacy and transcendence are on the lips of many. The Supreme Court alluded to this in its ruling on this issue. In speaking of the liberty and security of the person, the majority said, "A consideration of these interests cannot be divorced from the sanctity of life." The argument focused on "the generally held and deeply rooted belief in our society that human life is sacred." The Court maintained that autonomy must be balanced by the principle of the sanctity of life.

The Court's ruling made it clear that no longer will an individualistic view be the only one countenanced by the court. This will certainly be rubbished by those who assert that matters of faith and belief are only for personal or congregational privacy, but many are recognizing that issues of life and death cannot exclude the larger debate of purpose and essence. No one person's freedom is absolute. Taking the life or participating in taking the life of another is not one person's prerogative, be they friend, foe or physician.

And what about those who are extremely disabled? A possible result might be the attitude that, since we now have a legal provision that allows very sick people to take their lives and given the high cost of palliative care and the need for more available beds, those in such debilitating conditions have a responsibility to society to end their lives. Along with this possible outcome is the overarching concern that as a people we will lose our sense of obligation to pay the costs of those in need.

The community I represent has a deep commitment to the issue of life, an issue that calls for a national debate. But let us not be driven only by the physical distress of an individual or the tear of a politician. These are not a sound basis for an enormous shift in the way we view death and therefore life.

# 12

# When "Safe" Means "Danger"

S itting in a deck chair on the Titanic seems more reasonable than offering soothing assurance to young people that the use of a condom is their ticket to "safe sex."

Such language is reminiscent of Hollywood's "free love" lingo of the 1970s. Love – to one married, to the apostle Paul or to someone working in a hospice – is never "free" but costly. "Safe sex," like "free love," is an oxymoron – a contradiction in terms.

The current crusade promotes condoms to reduce the growing numbers of AIDS patients, illegitimate children and people being infected with sexually transmitted diseases (STDs). Implicit in the slick promos is the assurance that you can have all the fun you want, with whom you want, in whatever way you want, just as long as you use the latex cover-up.

What they do not tell us is how unsafe condoms really are in preventing pregnancy or disease. In a series of articles in the *Journal of the Society of Obstetricians and Gynaecologists of Canada*, Dr. Stephen J. Genuis, who practises medicine in Edmonton, documents the failure of condoms to prevent pregnancy and STDs, including AIDS.

First some facts: 50 percent of our population will acquire an STD by the age of 30 to 35. In North America, 12 million new cases are reported each year. Twenty percent of the female population between the ages of 14 and 40 harbour the human papilloma virus (HPV), a virus, says Genuis, which is unknown to many health professionals and for which there is no known cure. With this one virus alone there is a 50 percent chance it will be transmitted during a single sexual encounter. HPV and other STDs ripple their effects into adult life and for mothers, into the bodies and lives of their children.

AIDS is the most frightening of all STDs. With the delay (seven to 10 years) from infection to full-blown AIDS, we do not know what the numbers will be at the end of the century.

Now to the "safe sex" message of our governments, schools and national heroes. Described as the "vaccine" against catching diseases, condoms are designed to prevent contact between the skin of the partners and transmission of fluids. But how good are they?

Genuis's research shows that the average condom is 38 microns thick. (A rubber glove is 229 microns thick.) In the latex there are channels, five microns in width, penetrating the thickness of the covering. The sperm is five to seven microns thick and about 55 microns long; the hepatitis B virus is 0.5 microns and the HIV particle is only 0.1 micron.

A test of the strength of a condom found that there was a leakage of particles the size of an HIV particle in 29 out of 89 condoms tested. To give you a sense of the numbers of particles in sexually transmitted fluids, there are 100 million sperm for every one mL of seminal fluid and up to 10 trillion of the hepatitis B virus per mL of fluid. To claim that such microscopic particles can be prevented from transmission with a latex condom is like saying you can catch goldfish with a salmon net. But the possibility of transmission is not usually discussed on talk shows and is never covered in ads promoting "safe sex."

The possibility of STD, including AIDS, being transmitted during sexual activity is one part of the untold story. The numbers of young women becoming pregnant even while using condoms is the other part. Genuis refers to a study which suggests that more than half of female teenagers who insist their partners use a condom will be pregnant within three years of becoming sexually active.

A few years ago, Don Simmonds, national youth coordinator for the Canadian Baptist Federation, directed the True Love Waits campaign in Canada. It encouraged young people to pledge to their parents and each other that they will postpone sexual activity until marriage.

Simmonds expects that the failure of our educational programs and the promotion of the use of condoms will result in a wave of diseases and unwanted pregnancies. Then our society will be forced to face reality, not because of moral questions but because of the astronomical costs the diseases and unwanted pregnancies will place on society. It will become like smoking, he said. We'll be forced to find a better way.

Adults running public educational programs and government ad agencies who spend multi-million-dollar budgets of public money are derelict in their responsibility by not warning our youth that "safe sex" is a myth. In truth, it too often leads to heartache, disease and death.

As today we pay the price and witness the tragedy of hemophiliacs dying of AIDS because they were not warned by the Red Cross, in the years ahead our current youth – then adults – will cry out, "Why didn't you tell us the truth?"

The arguments of medical specialists like Genuis seem not to reach the pens of journalists or the rationale of public officials. Too often, it seems, they are anxious to ride the permissive behaviour bandwagon without shouting out the warning that as comfortable as the deck chairs seem, the ship is going down.

## 13

# The First Step to Healing

It was the first time I'd listened to a Christian Canadian native tell the story of being uprooted from his home as a child, put in a boarding school and left alone to struggle with growing up. I'd heard the same kind of story on radio or television, describing sad sagas of dislocation, but this time it was different. A brother in Christ was telling the story.

Absent in this account was the accusation that "it's all the white man's fault." I could see the five-year-old boy, yanked from the wilderness of his habitat, flown by a strange airplane to a foreign location and forced to live, confused and lonely, in a residence staffed by well-meaning but unaware religious people.

It did not take much effort for me to imagine the little fellow, hardly old enough to wash himself, crying lonely tears in the bunks of the institution.

Out of those years came confusion of identity, meaning and purpose. His fragmented young soul reacted in unruly behaviour, spinning the cycle of anger/reaction/hostility/reappraisal/alcohol/police/violence/jail.

This story was told at a consultation cohosted by World Vision and the Evangelical Fellowship of Canada, bringing to Winnipeg Christian leaders from the first nations/aboriginal community. We did this in response to the EFC general council's directive that we consider what might be done to encourage cooperation and fellowship within the native/aboriginal community.

In gentleness of spirit, we listened to their stories. We also talked about anger at "white people" and the often-underlying assumption that the aboriginal struggles are the result of the European invasion. But in the end we did begin to hear their heart. And what I heard forced me to reconsider.

Over the years I've heard various reasons given by non-native Canadians about why our native population is in such difficulty. I've had to work through these ideas, which unconsciously stratify like sediment in our thinking. Some of these popular cultural assumptions keep us from hearing the pain, let alone participating, in the Spirit's work of reconciliation.

These include myths of unending government largesse in treaty payments, welfare, educational and business grants, the natives' demands for compensation for huge tracts of land which seem inordinate, along with the complaint that historically the church – be it Roman Catholic, Anglican, or others – has robbed them of native spirituality.

I've heard these argued from both sides – the angry non-native critique and the bitter, native accusation and rebuttal. So who is right? Within these tensions I still have to ask myself the question, "How much longer will the arguments about the past stall me from pursuing the kingdom agenda for the future?" Though I may not be responsible for the world I inherit from a previous generation, I am responsible for the world I leave behind to the next generation.

## A New Ear to Hear

I've observed the United Church and others offer apologies to the native society for wrongs done to them in the name of Jesus Christ. My response has been that neither I nor the church I serve has, in my lifetime, done anything to hurt or demean natives as individuals or their society. So for me to ask them to forgive me was, in my view, only a kowtowing to the politically correct line. And that was not enough to draw me in.

During our meals, times of prayer, Bible study and reflection at the consultation, the Spirit of God helped me listen to something I had never heard before. It was a call they were making to be included.

I know that often in family disputes, one accuses the other of not listening. Usually the person being accused may be listening to the words, but is not hearing the real message. And that has been my problem. I've listened but not heard.

And what did I hear that day?

My sin was not of commission – I had not been part of a church that hauled children away to boarding schools. I've been secure in my rebuttal that my denomination and our evangelical church communities had no part in this tragic history – at least to the best of my knowledge.

But I did wake up to my sin: the sin of omission. It is not that I've done wrong; it is that I have not been about doing good. I've left them out of my prayers, love, friendships and time. First nations/aboriginal peoples are a part of our evangelical community but I haven't seen them that way. I know that theologically and in personal faith they are part of us. But in my living and ministry, I've left them out.

As we stood in a circle that night, I heard the Spirit speak so clearly that I could not avoid his words. In that moment my heart opened. We cried together. We hugged. We prayed. And we sang. The flood gates opened and we all sensed the work of Christ, calling us together in love and fellowship. It was a time of reconciliation and healing.

Understand that though many of our evangelical denominations have little or no ministry among the natives/aboriginals and those who are involved have a fairly recent and honourable history, many natives/aboriginals see the church all lumped in together, not divided by denominations or history. Here is a community that needs us and we need it. If part of being reconciled is for us to go the extra mile, then let it be done.

I'm reminded of a plaque my father had on the wall of his office: "Great Spirit, grant that I may not criticize my neighbour until I've walked two miles in his moccasins."

By God's help, I'm going to take my dad's prayer to heart.

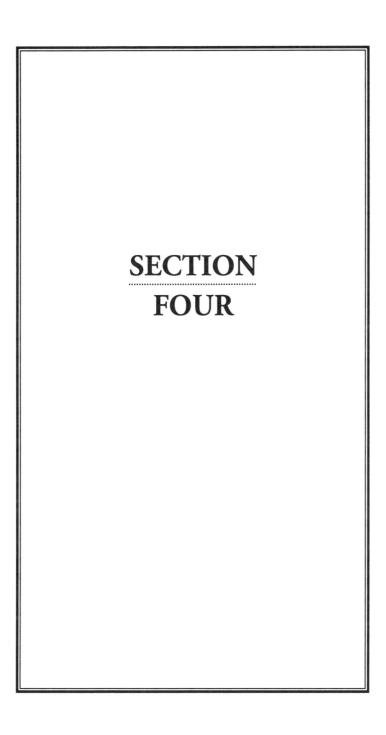

# SECTION
# FOUR

# 14

# In Search of the Evangelical Mind

To some people, "an intellectual evangelical" is an oxymoron – two contradictory ideas. Often a journalist assumes that evangelicals cannot cogently discuss the issues at hand.

Tragically it is too often true. We have been trapped by the notion that we best reflect our Lord by being proud about our lack of education. How often I have heard the argument, "After all, didn't the apostle Paul say, 'Not many of you were wise by human standards; not many were influential . . . But God has chosen the foolish things of the world to shame the wise. . . .' "

A gross misreading of what Paul said not only short-changes us on knowing about God's creation, but in terms of this country, we are unable to give leadership in such a way as to bring a godly, biblical mind to its rule.

Consistently, I am asked why the cultural gate-keepers do not reflect a biblical vision of life. Cultural pressures – including law, government policy and educational curricula – push our country away from giving any kind of recognition to faith.

But to complain of unfair treatment ignores what is obvious: people of faith have every opportunity of being in leadership. So why aren't we? It stems from two delusions: an uneducated mind is more fitting for faith and to give leadership in the world is to be worldly.

John Calvin, the 16th-century reformer, had something to

say about that. "By 'being fools' we do not mean being stupid. . . The profession of Christianity requires us to be immature, not in our thinking, but in malice. But do not let anyone . . . be swollen with pride . . . and so be quick to reject what he is told, indeed before he has sampled it."

In the early part of this century, much of the Protestant church succumbed to the dominant views of "higher criticism," which resulted in a liberal interpretation of the Scriptures, and to Darwinism, which attracted educators to a view of life and creation that ended up in discounting the existence of God. The tragic sidelining of Christian churches struck a note among those who reacted to the liberalizing shift. Going more for a religion of "the heart," they saw training of the mind as caving in to the world.

Today, evangelicals are tragically absent from having significant presence in critical contingents of culture. It is not a matter of gaining recognition or appreciation but of engaging many of the dominant ideologies that drive many Canadian policies and legislation and which are "no friend of grace."

A developed mind is not in opposition to biblical revelation. We can all tell stories of people who during their education turned from faith. But the same can be told of those who in the course of doing business, practising a profession or even in cultivating a relationship, walked away from Christ. Life in all arenas has a way of straining the chords of faith.

Although the apostle Paul said that one's pedigree does not measure one's wisdom, he was not degrading of the person, including the mind. Note Romans 1, in which he affirms the importance of being thoughtful.

If we continue to misrepresent what it means to follow Jesus by implying that one must be simple to believe, we debase his creation and get sidelined. Unless we take on the great, complex issues of our time, the gospel will simply not be there to inform, influence and shape.

Anger against school curricula may satisfy one's sense of outrage, but until we have Christians who are trustees, educational theorists and curriculum writers, all the outrage and letters of protest will count for little.

Stirring up the dust over genetic engineering may attract the press, but without Christians as geneticists, professors of ethics in our medical schools and scientists, we simply will flail at the wind with straws while the world marches by us.

Evangelical historian Mark Noll, in *The Scandal of the Evangelical Mind*, writes about the failure of evangelicals in this century (he is less hard on us in Canada) to engage our society with Christ's good news.

"For an entire Christian community to neglect, generation after generation, serious attention to the mind, nature, society, the arts – all spheres created by God and sustained from his own glory – may be, in fact, sinful," he writes.

Noll strikes at the centre of our dilemma. We want biblical faith to speak into our culture. But we will not be heard if all we do is holler out the message from the outside.

There is danger in any human enterprise. Pride in one's accomplishments strikes at the heart of faith, be it pride in a church building, economic affluence or the success of one's family. However, this fear of quality training and the preparation of the person – and the mind – keeps us from doing battle.

The mind and heart are equally God's creation. A mind without the heart is cold and unfeeling. A heart without a mind is, well, mindless.

An "evangelical mind" need not be an oxymoron.

# 15

# Thinking Christianly

Making sense of computers is an enormous challenge for me. I readily admit I'm a technological klutz. It takes a huge effort for me to read and make sense of computer software manuals. Now I'm on-line with "e-mail." From my computer, through the phone lines and out through the Internet system, I can send and receive messages from around the world. Just this morning my brother Dave sent a message via e-mail from Nizhny Novgorod, Russia.

However, unless I am given simple and explicit directions, I get absolutely lost if I have to figure out how a software system works. Why? Because I have not trained my mind to think in the world of computer technology.

Each of us has an area of interest in which we feel most comfortable. Clare, my car mechanic, knows what to look for when he puts his head under the hood. Lily, my wife, understands the notes on a sheet of music as she puts her hands to the piano keyboard. Juanita, our chief financial officer, can interpret the EFC's balance sheet. They have learned to make sense of their worlds of expertise.

To be a Christian means we are called to make sense of all of life within a view that comes from our comprehension of God's creation, our fallen world and his will.

Take angels, for example. In popular culture, especially that of European roots, there is a notion that angels exist in some mystical form. But the idea that angels are active and involved in our lives would be quite foreign, and indeed spooky, to most Canadians. People who have taken time to think Christianly know that angels are a normal and expected part of our everyday life. We cannot see them, but that does not mean they do not exist.

So, how do we come to think Christianly? Some people assume that the new birth automatically gives one a new mind. That is the beginning: "Therefore, if anyone is in Christ, he is a new creature; the old has gone, the new has come" (II Cor. 5:17). But that is just the beginning. It does not mean that our minds are automatically and instantly drafted so that we think Christianly. To do so requires discipline. Paul describes it this way: "Therefore I urge you, in view of God's mercy, to offer your bodies as living sacrifices, holy and pleasing to God – this is your spiritual act of worship. Do not conform any longer to the pattern of the world, but be transformed by the renewing of your mind. Then you will be able to test and approve what God's will is." (Rom. 12:1,2)

Offering our minds calls for daily exercise. It requires learning to see life through the eyeglasses of God's will. There is no easy way. It comes by consciously asking how God would call us to see life.

The most "natural" response of living in this age is to think within the boundaries of popular culture. The issue of headgear in Legion halls is a contentious question. Jews and Sikhs wearing their religious head coverings are not allowed in most Legion halls. Apart from the instinctive reaction to changing our traditions, for a Christian member of a Legion, the tough question is, what would Jesus say?

At the very centre of our life is the need to always and in every situation ask that very fundamental question. I am not suggesting that each of us will arrive at the same answer. God respects our individuality and personal journeys.

June 23 was declared taxation-free day. Someone has computed that all of our earnings so far this year equal what we will pay in taxes this year. Thus, what we earn after June 23 is the after-tax income. What is at the base of this fictitious day? An assumption that taxes are what the government takes from us. Though one could make a case that taxes in Canada are too high and though government need to be brought to task for the way they spend our money, the real danger is that we get sucked into the notion that taxation is a violation of our right to keep all we make.

A study of stewardship in the Scriptures gives evidence that everything we own is not ours. It is God's good gift to us. Enlightenment liberalism, while affirming the rights of the individual, pushes that notion beyond what biblical creation allows by describing life as made up essentially of the autonomous individual. But we are not alone. Life cannot be lived with only a view to "my rights." We live within God's creation, as people charged to live together. One of the ways we live together is by sharing resources for our protection, governing society and helping those who otherwise may be destitute.

So how does one think Christianly about this "taxation-free day?" Too easily we assume that the popular tax rebellion, because it opposes government spending, is somehow right and even "Christian."

Thinking Christianly calls for a refusal to assume that what is popular is biblical. One vulnerability of evangelicals, who sociologist Reg Bibby calls conservative Protestants, is to assume that if an idea fits the "conservative" point of view, it is therefore biblical.

To think as a Christian requires that our minds be fed from the Scriptures. This has a double impact. Our minds are "washed" by truth. The corroding assumptions that stick to our minds are challenged by the Word. Secondly, our minds are shaped by a new way of thinking. For example, the impulse of evangelicals to "take over" a society led by people who seem in opposition to anything Christian is modified by observing that Christ's path to the throne was by way of the cross.

Thinking Christianly does not happen automatically or easily. It is a discipline. I have to work at understanding why the computer reacts the way it does to my instruction. Likewise with thinking Christianly. The question is, do I spend as much effort in understanding God's view of the world as I do trying to understand Internet?

## 16

# Shutting off Bernardo

I t seems that every time I turn on the television or radio for news, there it is. Most newspapers and magazines have used it for front page coverage. And what is that? No, not the O.J. Simpson trial in Los Angeles. It is the Paul Bernardo trial in Toronto. It is ubiquitous. Almost inescapable.

Our world has become almost compulsive in its apparent need to fill time with horror stories of all kinds, examining the details in hours of excruciating boredom. It is as if our culture just cannot get enough of this stuff.

Last year this fascination got a kick start with the famous Bronco ride of O.J. Simpson. For months now, hours every day, viewers pore over who is right and wrong, making judgments on the clothes of the prosecutor or critiquing the defence when the lawyers do not get along. Even the CBC *Newsworld* now has a nightly roundup of the happenings in Los Angeles – proof, I suppose, that even good old mother CBC is not immune to the rabid demands of its Canadian viewers.

What is at the core of this inexhaustible thirst for gory details? Has life become so humdrum that at the end of a day we need to fill the vacuous state of modern existence with the lust, violence and abominable behaviour of infamous people? Is there no consciousness that the rapes and murders examined in the Simpson and Bernardo/Homolka trials actually did harm to teenagers and young women? While we stuff our barren souls with the screams induced by depraved minds, do we know what we are saying to ourselves, our friends, our culture and our God?

I have made up my mind. When the Bernardo trial is reported on radio I turn it off. When it comes on television I switch to another channel. When a paper or magazine puts it in my face I turn the page or push it aside.

Am I some sort of sensitive, shrinking soul who cannot face the gruesome stories of violence? I don't think so. Is it self-righteousness looking for a cause? No, I am too aware of my own fallenness and need of a Saviour. And my wife tells me I do not have a track record of turning away from conflict or the tough issues of life.

My reasons for saying "enough" to the murder stuff are these: First, I know enough to know what happened. I do not need more details to fill in the gaps. There has been sufficient detail to tell me of the dominance of evil and rule of violence.

But second, for me to countenance it any longer is as if I were a peeping Tom, eyeing through slits in the fence the anguish and sexual horrors of tragic victims and the deeds of unspeakable victimizers.

Also, much of life is filled with human tragedy. Every day our cities and towns and rural areas become hotbeds nursing the explosive nature of the human spirit out of touch with its creator and exacerbated by human fallenness. I do not need the details of the Bernardo trial to tell me more about that.

In May of 1968, I was ordained to ministry in a service in Brockville, Ont. Rev. Robert Argue preached the sermon and in it I recall his admonishing me and other ordinands to put a guard on our minds. He was right. I have learned that the eyes become the gateway, opening my mind to what I see; what I see I consider; what I consider I reflect on; what I reflect on I may come to believe; and what I believe I accept as being true. I cannot watch violence, be it a trial or a Hollywood special, and not be affected by it. It builds up until violence becomes acceptable. Like a frog in a pot of water, you never really know when the water is so hot as to snuff out life.

My calling is to preach and teach the gospel. To do that I need to be in touch with tragedy and bring to those I can a measure of strength and hope. But if I fill my life with the horrors of this trial, it will do the opposite. Instead of goodness, purity and holiness, the corrupting and corroding presence of ungodliness will pre-empt God's power and anointing.

Paul wrote, "For you were once darkness, but now you are light in the Lord. Live as children of light (for the fruit of the light consists in all goodness, righteousness and truth) and find out what pleases the Lord. Have nothing to do with the fruitless deeds of darkness, but rather expose them. For it is shameful even to mention what the disobedient do in secret." (Eph. 5:8-12)

Computer programers have an apt phrase: Garbage in, garbage out. We become what we read, see and hear. There comes a time in our inner life when the garbage of evil corrupts. The normal frictions of life are enough opportunity for my mind to absorb the opposite of God's life.

So for me, it has gone too far. The Bernardo trial is off limits.

# 17

# The Poor with us

I recall as a 10-year-old child going with my father to the southwest side of Saskatoon. It was winter and, as is sometimes the case in late December on the Prairies, it was cold.

The house was the kind that was one-storey, with half of the house in the ground and half out. I was surprised by what I saw as we walked down the stairs to the kitchen where the family who lived there was seated around the table. The floor was earthen. It took a moment for me to absorb that. No, my eyes were not deceiving me. There was no floor of wood or concrete. It was earth. Dirt. The family had a few rugs placed here and there. But there was no mistaking that the floor was earthen.

This was a family with whom we worshiped every Sunday at our church on 25th Street. Later, I went to high school with the family's eldest daughter. This was the early 1950s and the family was poor. The father had a job that paid very little. Government assistance hardly existed. In comparison, our modest minister's home seemed majestic.

I watched Dad as he graciously and without any spirit of condescension set down boxes of groceries and chatted with the family as he would with other friends. As equals we had prayer and then we left. They were an intact family: mom, dad and the children.

That was the kind of real poverty I remember as a young boy.

The family came to church and seemed to feel very much a part of the church family. The daughter – my classmate who always beat me in math – was slightly out on the social edge, but very much an equal to us all.

Would this family feel welcome in our churches today? Would they be comfortable walking through our doors and sitting in our pews? I look around in the churches I'm in and don't see many poor people in attendance. As I drive up in my late-model car I see the parking lots filled with other late-model cars. Though attire is becoming more casual in churches, the clothing is still of high quality. No, the poor seem either to go elsewhere or maybe to go nowhere at all. I wonder why.

The friends I move with have done quite well financially over the past few decades. We got our bumps in the last recession. But there is always a solid floor under us: no earth showing for us.

So how do I handle this issue? Do I resort to guilt? No. I've never believed that guilt as a motivator, apart from leading me to God and forgiveness, is of much value. But I do wonder about how we are dealing with the poor around us.

As our church community slowly climbed up the social and economic ladder from the early '60s to today, we in the community have assumed that those who are poor are either lazy, mentally challenged or unwise in their money management. That view might hold if there is work around. But we are living on the down side of a major economic revolution. The situation today, compared to that of the 1930s' depression, is less than parallel in its magnitude but is still similar. It wasn't that people didn't want to work then either; there was just not enough work to go around.

Look around at the new poor of this culture. Many tend to be mothers, single and alone. Before we conveniently slip into the argument that posits that they deserve their poverty – because they got pregnant while single, waste money on booze or are too lazy to find work – I want us to ask the question, what would

Jesus do?

No, that's not resorting to Bible thumping. At the heart of our kingdom faith, if we do not ask that question, we've become ideological believers and not pilgrims.

Government cutbacks are necessary. I hear no argument against that. The absolute dereliction of duty of past governments in piling up debt can no longer be ignored.

The welfare system is in shambles and needs reforming. I hear no dispute about this, including none from professionals who work with the poor. Welfare degrades, demotivates and dehumanizes people.

But that still leaves us with the question of what we as believers will do with the Christ who announced, "He has anointed me to preach good news to the poor." How will we deal with the prophet's call to "do away with the yoke of oppression; spend yourselves on behalf of the hungry; satisfy the needs of the oppressed?" And what will be the result? The prophet says, "You will be a well-watered garden, like a spring whose waters never fail."

Never in this century have evangelicals been so well off financially. We were poor. But as is often the case, the *nouveaux riches* quickly forget what it's like to be poor. This is our great moment to silence those who say the gospel is only for saving the "soul" and not the "person." The two, intertwined, call for salvation, healing and restoration.

In our churches may we be creative, helping and motivating. In our personal lives may we be caring, loving and personally attached to a person or family struggling with poverty. The poor invite us to show Christ's grace.

## 18

# Worldliness

What is worldliness? To answer this question personally takes us back to the fundamental question of how one sees life; that is, one's world view. I was raised in a church community that defined "worldliness" in very specific ways. For example, smoking, drinking and movie attendance were seen as worldliness – for specific reasons. Though we didn't understand the relationship of smoking to health, smoking was associated with those who weren't willing or interested in submitting to the Lordship of Christ as smoking was addictive. Drinking was clearly the reason for societal ills; and movies were a corrupting influence. Thus we were warned to stay away from such entertainment and life-style issues, which came from those who had no interest in promoting a biblical view of life. Though such a view of worldliness was very narrow, it did establish in my mind an understanding of the tension of two worlds: the world of Christ's kingdom and the world of the "deceiver."

To unwrap this commonly misunderstood term, "the world," first we'll look at how the Bible refers to it, what it does not mean and then at how we can construct a working definition for today.

References to "the world" in the Bible:

"They are the ungodly, that prosper in the world; they increase in riches." (Psa. 73:12, KJV)

"The care of this world, and the deceitfulness of riches, choke the word." (Matt.13:22, KJV)

"If the world hates you, keep in mind that it hated me first. If you belonged to the world, it would love you as its own. As it is, you do not belong to the world, but I have chosen you out of the world." (John 15:18,19)

"For the wisdom of this world is foolishness in God's sight." (I Cor. 3:19)

"The god of this world has blinded the minds of unbelievers, so that they cannot see the light of the gospel." (II Cor. 4:4)

"As for you, you were dead in your transgressions and sins, in which you used to live when you followed the ways of the world and of the ruler of the kingdom of the air, the spirit who is now at work in those who are disobedient." (Eph. 2:1,2)

"Set your minds on things above, not on earthly things." (Col. 3:2)

"The love of money is a root of all kinds of evil." (I Tim. 6:10)

"For Demas, because he loved this world, has deserted me." (II Tim. 4:10)

"Such wisdom does not come down from heaven, but is earthly, unspiritual, of the devil." (James 3:15)

". . . don't you know that friendship with the world is hatred toward God?" (James 4:4)

"Do not love the world or anything in the world. If anyone loves the world, the love of the Father is not in him. For everything in the world – the cravings of sinful man, the lust of his eyes, and the boasting of what he has and does – comes not from the Father but the world." (I John 2:15-16)

As Jesus was giving his famous Sermon on the Mount, his telling line on what he expected of his followers was "Don't be like them" (Matt. 6:8). John Stott, in his book *Christian Counter Culture*, says, "Jesus emphasized that his true followers, the citizens of God's kingdom, were to be entirely different from others.

They were not to take their cue from the people around them, but from him, and so to prove to be genuine children of their heavenly father."

There is clearly the distinction between the attitudes, values and behaviour as determined by Satan in contrast to that which comes from God. Our failure to determine what is or is not worldliness, is because we based it primarily on certain forms of behaviour, forgetting about attitude and values.

### What it is not

Worldliness does not mean the physical world. Planet Earth is God's creation. "The earth is full of the goodness of the Lord." (Psa. 33:5)

When it was created, God looked at it and said, "It is good." Subsequent to creation, sin entered into all of human life, which includes the earth. But that is not to say that the earth and its products are worldly.

Worldliness does not mean the physical body. Made in God's image, the human body, though also infected by sinfulness, is the body of God's creation. John shocked those who believed that the body was evil when he said, "The Word (Jesus) was made flesh and made his dwelling among us" (John 1:14). People do use their bodies to serve something other than God, but that is not to say the human body is itself worldly.

John's reference to "the lust of the flesh" is exactly that: that which arises out of the body under the influence of lust. Paul went so far as to remind us that our bodies are "temples" of God. God takes up residence in this physical construct known as the body.

Neither does worldliness mean living in the world. Living in the world does not mean that the very act of living is worldly, for it is in the context of living that the very life of Jesus is experienced. As well, it is in living that we do warfare with evil.

The drama of God recreating all of life is played out on the stage of life.

Worldliness does not refer to the gifts and abilities of people. Abilities are part of creation, distributed so society can function. Not all of us are artists. Not all are leaders. We do not all have expertise in business. Not all are able counselors or teachers or scientists or builders. Though Paul specifically refers to the gifts operating within the church (Rom. 12:6-8), these gifts also are part of people, whatever they believe. These can be used for good or evil. But the gifts themselves and the very owning of them are his creation. Thus, even people who have no allegiance to God can, by the use of their gifts, glorify God.

Worldliness does not mean living in time. Time is God's creation. "In the beginning" tells us so. We do not know what would have been God's strategy and the plan of time if there had been no entry of sin. But we do know that time is of God's doing. Even though we are promised the end of time and the fullness of eternity, the present time is of God's creation.

Worldliness is not synonymous with the Earth, physical life or human experience.

## A Working Definition

But what is worldliness? Worldliness means giving preferred status to something other than God. It is setting up anything in life above devotion and obedience to God. When Moses was absent from the people, receiving the Ten Commandments, his brother Aaron crafted a golden calf, giving people something to worship. The golden calf became a symbol for worship over the creator, making it an idol.

Worldliness means allowing concerns to overcome faith. It was "by faith" that Abraham heard and obeyed the voice of God. If there is anything central to Christianity it is faith. By which I mean living with the belief that what God said, he meant, and that our very lives can be lived on it. If one's fear of insufficient funds gets in the way of trusting God, that problem is worldly.

Worldliness means caring about life without regard to eternity. Because we are people of time we think in terms of time. Entering into adulthood, we look ahead and chart a course that will lead us to whatever we decide is important. This is valid and appropriate, but it's not all. We also know that God's will is for his people to live on into eternity. To fail to compute that into the equation of what I do is to miss a vital element of his kingdom. If my objectives in living do not keep in mind my ultimate destination, these objectives have become worldly.

Worldliness means ignoring what concerns God. God has not given us a little red book that says, "One to ten, here is what concerns me." But the Bible is a faithful record of his working with people throughout history. And within that interaction we discover his concerns. He told the people of Israel what he required of them, "to do justice, to show mercy and to walk humbly before their God." These are very specific terms of concern. If the running of my business involves only "the bottom line" and leaves out God's concerns, my business has become worldly.

Worldliness means putting oneself first over others. Popular to our culture is making a sports team number one. This drive to be successful – which often means at the expense of others – can be the essence of worldliness. That is not to say we must not strive to be successful. But we are called to "love your enemies and pray for those who persecute you." (Matt. 5:43) If getting ahead requires my stepping on others, my success reflects worldliness.

Worldliness means preoccupation with being religiously correct. There is a tendency on the part of those who are deeply committed to faith to emphasize being correct. In Jesus' day it was the Pharisees. Today it is can be religious fundamentalists. Because of the shifting of some away from a biblically driven vision of life, those who want a more focused biblical faith will be overcome with the need to be always "correct." This leads to a proud and exclusive spirit. If holding on to my faith means intolerance of people with whom I disagree, that faith is in its essence worldly.

Worldliness means worshipping the gifts instead of the giver. Some people thank God for their abundance and then go on living as if what they have is all there is to life. Thankfulness is the opposite. It means knowing that whatever we have is not ours by rights but his; we manage these gifts as stewards, not owners. If my car, house or belongings become something else than a gift, they become worldly.

Worldliness means being driven by ideas outside of the kingdom. Worldliness is that which overrides the essential element of God's concern, which is the agenda of the king, Jesus Christ. The Sermon on the Mount is explicit, definitive and all encompassing. We need only ask ourselves, after a reading of this passage, "What would be the concern and action plan of Jesus?" If my attitudes, aspirations, behaviour and relationships are not in line with the concerns of Christ's kingdom, then they are worldly.

Is Jesus, therefore, not concerned with the world? He said, "God so loved the world. . . ." Is there a contradiction? Some suggest that what Jesus was saying was that God loved the people of the world but wasn't concerned with other facets of the world. But we hear Jesus praying to the Father:

"I have given them Thy word; and the world has hated them, because they are not of the world, even as I am not of the world."

"I do not ask Thee to take them out of the world, but to keep them from the evil one."

"They are not of the world, even as I am not of the world." (John 17:14-16)

What in the world does he mean?

Could it mean that Jesus only interest is the "souls" or spiritual aspect of life? One would ask, why did he show such concern over the physical needs of people? Was it just as a means to an end, to establish his credentials as God? This seems strange for one who harshly judged those who used means and justified them by the end result. Jesus seemed to authentically care for those distressed by sickness and even death.

The obvious conclusion is that Jesus is concerned with the world. He said, "God so loved the world. . . ." and his prayer to the Father makes it clear that his vision for his people was to serve faithfully in the world.

Jesus loves the world and all creation upon it. Worldliness is a position of the heart in which an aspect of the creation supercedes the creator. As his people we can celebrate his world while avoiding being wordly.

# 19

# The Ultimacy of Truth

On a recent David Letterman evening television program, Madonna, the very popular icon of this generation was his guest. Her two activities were first to persuade him to examine undergarments she had thrown on his desk and then to convince him of the therapeutic value of urine for athlete's foot in the shower. This modern star, thought to be the wealthiest singer today, stunned even the usually unflappable Letterman. In his futile attempt to get her off of the set, he finally began talking to her. While my wife and I were dismayed by her behaviour, the irony of the evening came when she turned her insolent face into his and asked, "Why can't you ask me any questions about me and my life?" It seemed either it had not occurred to Letterman to ask questions of substance or that he didn't have any to ask. Though some would decry Madonna, that night we all saw the culturally bankrupt trivia Letterman has to sell.

That is part of our world. In that world we live and work out our calling and faith.

Grandpa Stiller emigrated from Sweden in the late 1800s and settled in the Swedish community of Minnedosa, Manitoba. Out of the famine and hardships of the Scandinavian world, he entered the harsh west, built a sod hut, married an immigrant from his home country and began to work the land. The winters were cruel and the mosquitoes were almost enough to lift one off the ground with their wide, whirring blades.

Out of that family my brothers and sisters and I were raised in the humble but elegant province next door – Saskatchewan. Our home was simple, with a deep sense of trust in God. We were kept "from the world." Much of what our friends at school did for entertainment, we couldn't. But we had hay rides. Thank God for hay rides. We never felt life was passing us by.

Then on to university in the 1960s. As a student, in the midst of the swirl of the "God is dead" debates, I wondered if the faith I had learned at my mother's knee was, as Francis Schaeffer put it, "true truth" or had it been just a placating and warm-fuzzy answer, stilling my child-like questions of life. Would those gentle answers from a loving mother carry the really big questions: Who am I? What am I worth? Where am I going?

Somehow I made it through and now, as we look into the future, what do we see?

This era is labelled by some as post-modern. Academic arguments will be debated over what that really means, but we know we live in a modern world that continues to shift, turn and change. Our western world has been shaped by technology, urbanization, modern communication, travel, mass production and science and medicine.

Undergirding this explosion of ideas is liberal individualism, a belief in the autonomy and the invincibility of the human will. "What can't we do?" we arrogantly ask. And yet we aren't sure. Faced with the excess of our success, we gulp and burp on the indulgence of a western world, determined to still live by the message of the 1980s which was, "more is best and the bigger it is the more it's preferred."

With the horrors of previous decades staring us in the face, a recent car add says it well, "Why follow anyone again?" Is there anyone you can trust? The theme of my generation was, "Don't trust anyone over 30." That is, until we were 30. Then it became the refrain of the generation following us.

So whom do you trust? Deconstructionists and post-modernists disclaim any notion of truth, except that which exists in the search for one's own therapeutic well-being. Eliminating historical or objective truth as only that which exists by the will of person, truth becomes only opinions, and principles become nothing more than preferences.

Debunking rationality and abandoning any search for truth, we turn instead to believe that the management of self and the environment is all there is, as we press to the goal of well-being. Believing that self is all there is and that it is the very centre of existence, Alister MacIntyre writes its epitaph, "Truth has been replaced as a value and replaced by psychological effects."

With the debunking of truth as a reality – that is apart from the internal self – we lose ourselves in the frenzy of self discovery. When you no longer believe the Northern Star is fixed and can be trusted as a point to guide your ship, the only stars we can now admit to being reality are those within our selves.

And so Madonna, in her seemingly desperate search for recognition and her need to be more radical and scandalous than before, looks into the face of a neatly dressed and well-spoken friend of the late night set and asks, "Can't you even ask me something of importance?"

My question is, if the autonomous, liberal, individualistic self of modernity has not brought us the greatness of life we long for and the deconstruction of post modernists discount the possibility of there being any such thing as truth, where does this generation turn?

Jesus and Pilate stood nose to nose. The two most obvious powers were locked in battle. Pilate in that moment, and I assume with an air of exasperation, asked, "What is truth?" As a military specialist, trying to make sense of the religion and of the politics of Judea, he must have been confused. In his strategy of placating the feelings of the most vocal leaders and yet winning the commendation of Caesar as a competent and fair leader, he must have often asked himself, "What in the world is really true after all?" Even a hard-nosed, utilitarian, battle-worn general would realize that there are issues of truth which confuse and yet compel us.

Jesus lost. At least that's what the boys in the streets were saying. But that was not the end of the matter. History tells a more complete – and yet not fully complete – story. (There is more to come.) Pilate lost. Yet today we are compelled to work out what Jesus would do. Being smug in the ultimate victory of Christ does not help us in working out what we should do now. The world changes quickly. Generation after generation is forced to seek its own way of responding to the classical concern about what is true. That challenge has become even more focused.

Two factors have made that so: first the twentieth-century assumption that we can engineer and construct our world has fallen just as surely as the Berlin wall fell. But that assumption of social engineering was supported by more than just supporters of a Marxist ideology. Conservative and right-wing governments, operating out of a secular mind, have believed that their social engineering departments ultimately could solve human problems.

The second factor is the enormous burden of human need. The angst of the modern human heart is beyond understanding. Look around you:

• Rwanda: an unbelievable death rate. Out of vicious tribal warfare, corruption and evil, people die even as I speak.

• The fragmented old Yugoslavia: who are we to believe? Is it the Croats, the Serbs? Are so-called Christians performing the ethnic cleansing of Muslims? Just watch the evening news, if you dare, and then wonder what hurt is about.

• The Labrador island, a place to which former "enlightened" federal and provincial governments moved native peoples: today we see darkly into the souls of children and teenagers who out of the exhaustion of their futility, breath in noxious fumes, if not to end this vale of tears in death, at least to numb the mind for just a few hours.

• A counselor told me it is safer for many little girls to be on the streets of our towns and cities than to be at home in their beds tonight.

This is not being melodramatic.

I call you to look at the world around you and ask the question of Pilate. "What is truth?"

Given the western world, under the assumptions of both post Enlightenment thought and post modernists cannot bring this generation an underlying understanding of reality, I believe the thesis of Proverbs 16:3 can. "Commit to the Lord whatever you do, and your plans will succeed."

This verse has three poignant messages: First, you commit only to one you trust because you believe in the integrity of the person's being. A child tucking a sweaty palm into the hand of a parent, without looking either way, willingly trusts the parent to see her across the busy street.

Second, in the light of the one you trust, your actions are shaped. You won't hand over to a trustworthy person something of questionable worth. For committing implies approval and approval calls for careful thought as to what is important not only for yourself but for the one you trust.

Third, success is then defined, not by the hawkers of Bay street or the marketers of television infomercials but by the eternal reality of a God who, in love, both created and redeemed.

Don't be trapped by the cultural wrappings of your generation. See further than that. Don't trust the many voices of post-cultural thought, who in their essence are nothing more than the babblings of the sorcerer's apprentices. Don't live in fear of the unknown, afraid of a future which in the language of this age is pointless.

A story that compels me to live and die for truth comes from the early centuries of the Christian era.

A young monk named Telemachus wanted, more than anything else, to visit the Holy See in Rome. Receiving permission from his bishop, he wended his way southward into Rome. When he arrived, he was surprised that the streets were empty. He called to a lone man walking a side street and asked, "Where is everyone?"

The shopkeeper recognized the young cleric must be from out of town.

"The great gladiator fights are on at the Coliseum," he said. "Follow me."

As they got closer to the Coliseum, the monk could hear the crescendo of noise as people cheered on their favourite gladiator. Telemachus still did not understand; he had never seen or heard of a gladiator fight before.

As he walked into the Coliseum he saw two men fighting. At last he understood. They were trying to kill each other. Within moments one of the combatants slipped and the other, now obviously the victor, was about to plunge his sword into his adversary. He stopped, paused and looked up at Caesar, waiting for the sign as to whether his opponent should live or die. Caesar turned to the bloodthirsty crowd around him – looking for their answer – who cried for blood. Caesar turned to the gladiator and gave the thumbs down sign. Death.

In the meantime, Telemachus had rushed down into the arena. The gladiator plunged his sword into what he thought was his defeated opponent. But, unknown to him, the young monk had slipped in between the two gladiators and it was he who received the mortal blow.

Tradition tells us that a transfixing silence fell across the bloodthirsty crowd; in one shocking moment, they realized what they were doing and what was going on. They all left without a sound, from what was to be the last gladiator fight ever waged in the Coliseum in Rome.

At the cost of his life, in a simple and profound way, Telemachus faced the assumptions of his generation. He wanted to live with a mindset that affirms that success is defined by the ultimacy of what is true. If we choose to live by the standards of success measured not by our popular culture nor by the current wave of philosophers, but the gospel of our risen Jesus, the outcome may be different than what we imagined, but the success of our life will be assured.